Opening the West

Rosemary Neering

Canada
A People's History

THOMSON
★
NELSON

Australia   Canada   Mexico   Singapore   Spain   United Kingdom   United States

THOMSON

NELSON

Canada: A People's History
Opening the West

Series Consultants
Donald Bogle, Don Quinlan

Author
Rosemary Neering

Director of Publishing
Beverley Buxton

General Manager, Social Studies, Business Studies, and Languages
Carol Stokes

Publisher, Social Studies
Doug Panasis

Managing Editor, Development
Karin Fediw

Product Manager
Nadia McIlveen

Senior Editor
Susan Petersiel Berg

Editorial Coordinator
Amy Hingston

Executive Director, Content and Media Production
Renate McCloy

Director, Content and Media Production
Lisa Dimson

Production Manager
Cathy Deak

Senior Production Coordinator
Kathrine Pummell

Interior and Cover Design
Daniel Crack, Kinetics Design

Photo Research
Lisa Brant, Alene McNeill

Printer
Transcontinental Printing Inc.

Canadian Broadcasting Corporation Representative
Karen Bower

The authors and the publisher are grateful to the Canadian Broadcasting Corporation for its assistance in the preparation of this volume in the book series based on its 17-episode, bilingual television documentary series, *Canada: A People's History*. For more information about *Canada: A People's History*, please visit www.cbc.ca/history.

Contents

INTRODUCTION

THE BIG IDEA

In 1867, when the colonies of Canada West, Canada East, New Brunswick, and Nova Scotia united to become the Dominion of Canada, the West was the domain of Native people, Métis, and fur traders. The great North West, lying between the Canadian Shield and the Rockies, was either controlled by the Hudson's Bay Company or directly by Britain. One small settlement on the Red River, near present-day Winnipeg, was home to several thousand Métis and a handful of fur traders and Canadians. On the west coast, a gold rush had brought thousands of people to the mainland, and towns had grown up on Vancouver Island, on the Fraser River, and in the Cariboo.

In 1867, the North West was home to about 30 000 Native people and 10 000 Métis.

TIMELINE

1869 Canada takes over Rupert's Land and North-Western Territory

Louis Riel leads Red River Rebellion

Smallpox devastates First Nations

1858 Gold Rush in B.C.

James Douglas named governor of B.C.

1871 B.C. joins Confederation

1867 Confederation

1870 Execution of Thomas Scott

Manitoba joins Confederation

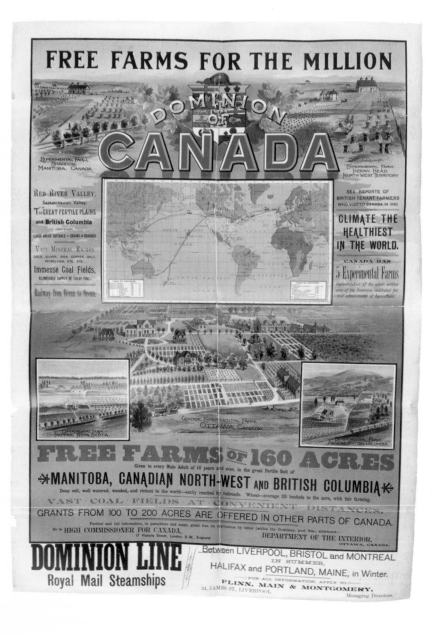

At the time of Confederation, there was little contact between the few people living in this great expanse of prairies, forests, mountains, and coast and the Canadians in the east. But that was about to change. The new government of Canada had bold plans for a country that stretched from sea to sea. It would take over the North West and expand all the way to the coast. Its ambitious scheme included a transcontinental railway and thousands of new settlers. What it did not include was respect for the **rights** of the Métis and First Nations people who already lived in the West.

Canada's first step into the West landed the new country in the middle of a dramatic conflict when Louis Riel and the Métis rebelled against the government's plans in 1869. The government stumbled again when it failed to negotiate **treaty** rights with the First Nations on the west coast, and again when it failed to keep its promises to the First Nations on the prairies.

TIMELINE

Louis Riel

1885 Riel leads Northwest Rebellion

Last Spike completes CPR

Riel hanged for treason

Sir John A. Macdonald

1874 North-West Mounted Police arrive in the West

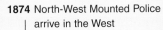

1873 P.E.I. joins Confederation

Cypress Hills Massacre

Pacific Scandal

1876 Treaties signed with First Nations

1891 Death of Sir John A. Macdonald

PICTURE THIS

Imagine how you would feel if strangers suddenly took over your school-yard and started building houses and grocery stores. This is the kind of situation the Métis and First Nations people faced when the government of Canada began offering settlers free land in the West.

What rights do people have when new-comers move into the place where they live? How should Native people be treated when they are reduced to a small minority of the population? Do people have a right to a voice in decisions that affect their lives? How do we make sure all regions in Canada are fairly treated? These questions were central in the opening of the West. They are still part of the bigger question of what it means to be a Canadian.

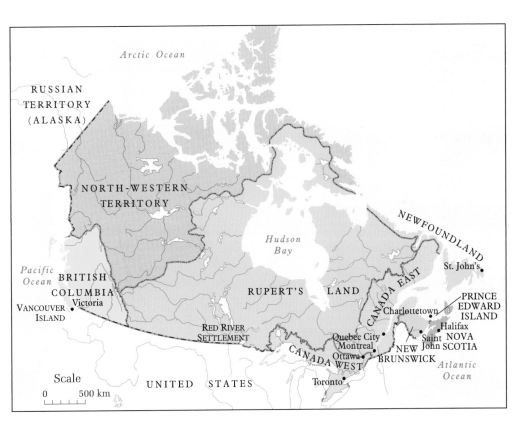

Canada and the West in 1867

SETTING THE SCENE

The Choices

British Columbia had a number of choices for its political future: union with Canada, remaining a British colony, or union with the United States. British Columbians made their decision based on promises that Canada offered to them. The North West had no such choice: the land was turned over to Canada without consulting the people who lived there. They had to decide how to make sure that Canada heard their voices. Canada, too, had choices to make. How would Native people be treated? How could Canada keep control of the North West? How did the North West fit into its political and economic future?

Change and Conflict

The North West and British Columbia underwent massive change in the 1870s and 1880s. The buffalo that sustained the Native people and the Métis were all killed off. New settlers arrived, and took over land already used by First Nations and Métis. A railway was built across the land. Many newcomers thought the Native people and Métis were inferior and deserved no rights. Conflict was inevitable. In the American territories to the south, wars against the Native people resulted in thousands of deaths. How would a similar conflict play out in western Canada?

Hunting buffalo in the North West, mid-1800s

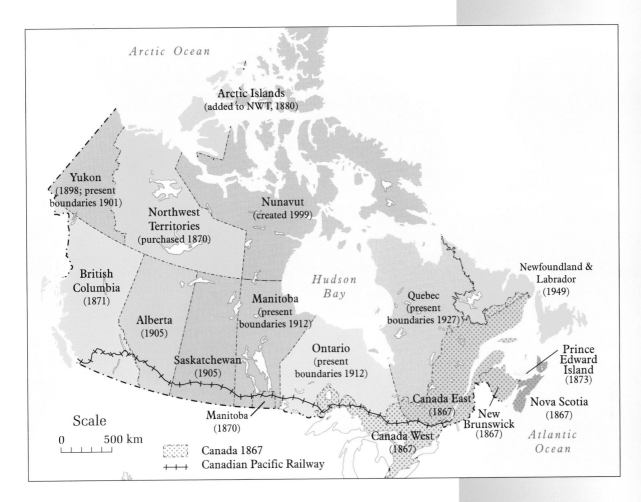

THE AFTERMATH

Do these events that happened more than a hundred years ago really matter? Why should we care about how Native people were treated, or why people came to the West? Is it important to know how governments acted in the past?

Many of the issues that trouble Canadians today are rooted in decisions and resentments from yesterday. In British Columbia, governments and First Nations continue to argue about treaties—because no treaties were signed in the nineteenth century. Today, some people in the West are unhappy about their role in Canada. Knowing how that role came about may help all Canadians understand the West better.

We are a nation of immigrants, and even today, we seek better understanding between people who have lived here for a long time and new Canadians. Knowing the stories of people who have immigrated here over the years may help us understand where we all fit in this greater story of Canada.

Today, Canada stretches from sea to sea. This map shows when the provinces and territories joined Confederation. In the West, Manitoba was the first to join in 1870, followed by British Columbia in 1871. The provinces of Saskatchewan and Alberta were carved out of the old North-Western Territory in 1905.

Telling Their Stories

THOMAS D'ARCY McGEE

Thomas D'Arcy McGee was born in Ireland in 1825 and immigrated to the United States in 1842, along with thousands of other Irish families. He returned to Ireland in 1845 and became involved in plans for an Irish rebellion against Britain. When he immigrated to Montreal in 1857, he turned against violence and was elected as a representative for Canada East in the Legislative Assembly of the United Province of Canada. McGee had a talent for getting along with all of the politicians in the legislature. He believed that the people in the colonies of British North America could work together to build a nation, despite their differences. He spoke eloquently in support of Confederation at the conferences in Charlottetown and Quebec in 1864, and his beliefs had a strong effect on John A. Macdonald. Watch *Canada: A People's History*, Episode 9: "From Sea to Sea" (16:04:25 to 16:13:02). Discuss with a classmate how you think McGee's assassination in 1868 affected the way John A. Macdonald dealt with change and conflict during his years as prime minister.

◀ Playback ▶

1. Briefly describe the inhabitants of the North West in 1867.

2. What political choices did the people in British Columbia face in 1867?

3. Why should Canadians today care about events that happened in the past in the Canadian West?

CHAPTER I

RED RIVER AND MANITOBA

On a late July day in 1869, a dark-haired, 24-year-old man gazed with love and pride at the land and family he had left 11 years ago. Louis Riel was home. This Métis son of Red River was much changed from the shy schoolboy who had headed east to Montreal a decade earlier. Now he was fluent in English as well as French. He had learned from his study of the law and politics to argue well, and he knew as much about the outside world as anyone at Red River.

His country had also changed. No longer the home of just the Métis and fur traders, it now housed Canadians who saw easy pickings in the West and who scorned both Métis and Native people. Louis Riel had come home—just in time to play a leading role in the drama that was about to overtake the West.

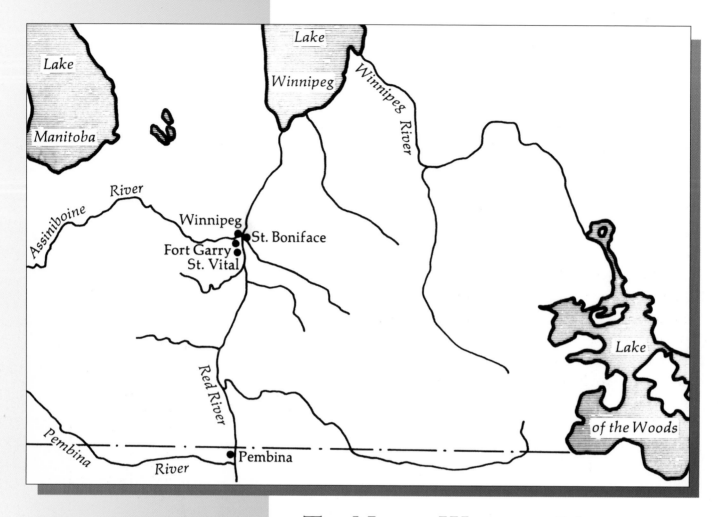

The Red River area in the North West, near present-day Winnipeg

THE NORTH WEST IN 1869

The Land

In 1670, Charles II, the British king, assigned the territory drained by "all the rivers that run down to Hudson's Bay" to the Hudson's Bay Company and called it Rupert's Land. The governors of the company wanted control over the vast region so they could make a profit from trading furs. The king wanted to be sure that the northern half of the continent was under British, not French, control. Beyond the wide horseshoe surrounding Hudson Bay, between the Arctic Ocean and the Rocky Mountains, was the uncharted North-Western Territory, which Britain also claimed.

Two hundred years later, the land was much more clearly defined. Britain had put an end to French territorial claims. Explorers and mapmakers had travelled across the region. Britain and the United States had agreed on the **49th parallel** as the border between their territories.

The People

About 25 000 Native people ranged across the plains and forests. They were members of the great nations of Ojibwa, Cree, Assiniboine, Blackfoot, and Chipewyan. A network of fur forts lay along the rivers between Hudson Bay and the Rockies. The furs traders did not encourage settlement, for they realized that settlers would interfere with trade.

About 13 000 people lived in the Red River area. A majority of them were Métis—the descendants of marriages between white fur traders and Native women. The larger group of Métis were of French and Native origin; a smaller number were of British and Native origin.

Also at Red River were the men of the Hudson's Bay Company, headquartered at Fort Garry, and families descended from Lord Selkirk's Scottish and English settlers. Rounding out the settlements along the river were a few hundred Canadians, who had come to Red River expecting that Canada would soon take over Rupert's Land.

Traditional lands and names of First Nations in Canada

Hudson's Bay Company fur-trading fort in Rupert's Land

Free Trade

In 1849, a group of Métis poured out of the Fort Garry courthouse, shouting their delight: "Le commerce est libre!" One of them, Guillaume Sayer, had stood trial for trading outside the **monopoly** held by the Hudson's Bay Company. He was found guilty, but received no punishment because he had so many supporters in the colony.

According to the agreement between Great Britain and the Hudson's Bay Company, the company had exclusive trading rights in all of the North West. But many of the Métis who lived at Red River wanted to trade their own furs and goods, particularly with American settlements to the south. Now, anyone could trade furs, **pemmican**, and any other goods. The power of the Hudson's Bay Company had been broken.

CANADA BUYS RUPERT'S LAND

"It shall be lawful for the Queen ...
on address from the Houses of Parliament of Canada,
to admit Rupert's Land and the
North-Western Territory,
or either of them, into the Union."
— BRITISH NORTH AMERICA ACT, 1867

When its trading **monopoly** was broken in 1849, the Hudson's Bay Company lost interest in governing the vast North West. Some people at Red River wanted to join Canada. Others thought that union with the U.S. was a better idea. Most simply wanted to be consulted about any new deal and to set conditions under which they would become citizens of a new country.

They were ignored. In 1869, without talking to the people of the North West, Canada bought Rupert's Land from the Hudson's Bay Company for $1.5 million, agreeing that the company could keep one-twentieth of the most fertile land and continue to trade "without hindrance or exceptional taxation." Britain also turned over the rest of the North West to Canada.

Why Did Canada Want the North West?

- Vast tracts of good farming land would attract new settlers.
- Immigrants would create a new market for products from eastern Canada.
- Canada needed Rupert's Land and the North West to realize its dream of a country that stretched from sea to sea and to prevent the U.S. from taking over the area.

Why Did the United States Want the North West?

- Some Americans thought the U.S. had a **"manifest destiny"** to control the whole continent of North America.
- New land would become available for settlers.
- Money could be made by selling American products to the North West.

"THE SITUATION."—See next page.

This cartoon was on the cover of a Montreal magazine in 1870. Out in the cold of winter, Miss Red River must choose between the clearly evil Uncle Sam at the U.S. Hotel and the welcoming Mrs. Britannia at Hotel Canada.

◄ Playback ►

1. What changes did the right to trade freely bring to people in the West?

2. Why was the Hudson's Bay Company ready to sell Rupert's Land?

3. What were some similar reasons why Canada and the U.S. wanted to own Rupert's Land?

4. What was the main difference in their reasons for owning Rupert's Land?

THE DRAMA AT RED RIVER

"The people cannot tolerate the idea of having been sold ..."
— ALEXANDRE TACHÉ, BISHOP OF RED RIVER

Scene 1: Stopping the Surveyors

Before Canada officially acquired Rupert's Land, Prime Minister John A. Macdonald sent Canadian surveyors to **survey** the land around the Red River settlement. They used the American system of dividing land. With the 49th parallel as a base line, they planned to carve the territory into squares that could be claimed by settlers.

Many of the Métis had lived at Red River for generations. They already had their own land, surveyed according to the system in Quebec, where long narrow lots fronted on the river. After peacefully surveying land nearer the American border, the surveyors reached Métis land and laid their chains across one of the lots. The French-speaking owner was unable to make them understand that the land was already taken. The Métis galloped off for help. Ninety minutes later, 16 horsemen dismounted and surrounded the surveyors. One stood firmly on the surveyors' chain. Their leader, Louis Riel, told them in English to depart: "You go no further. This land belongs to Monsieur Marion."

A Canadian surveying crew sets up camp

Scene 2: Blocking the Governor

Back in Canada, Prime Minister Macdonald had decided that there would be no **self-government** in the North West. Instead, a lieutenant governor and an appointed council would control the region. Macdonald appointed William McDougall to take on the post of lieutenant governor as soon as Canada officially took over the land. McDougall was not a wise choice. He was anti-French, anti-Catholic, arrogant, and mean-spirited. The Métis feared he would put his own followers—who were English, Protestant, and Canadian—in positions of power.

McDougall took a route through the United States to get to his new post at Red River. With him was a large entourage of servants and followers, as well as 60 wagons filled with supplies. The Métis knew that McDougall had no official status until Canada's deal was signed. Led by Louis Riel, they blocked the only trail north from the United States into Red River.

On the day Canada was supposed to take possession of the North West, McDougall read the proclamation at the U.S. border. He did not know that Prime Minister Macdonald had decided that, before taking over the North West, Canada needed to resolve its differences with the people of Red River. Six weeks later, a defeated McDougall returned to Canada.

Fort Garry

Scene 3: Occupying Fort Garry

The rumour swept through Red River: the Canadians were planning to occupy Fort Garry. It was filled with guns, food, and supplies—all the things Louis Riel needed for his own men. In just a few minutes, Riel and a hundred men took over the fort. They needed the fort for three reasons: to keep the Canadians from taking command, to have access to supplies, and to make the Canadian government take them seriously. By taking over the fort, they effectively ended the rule of the Hudson's Bay Company in the North West.

List of Rights

These are some of the rights the Métis demanded as conditions for joining Canada:

- the power to elect their own legislature
- free homesteads and a law to protect their land
- a railway to Winnipeg within five years
- payment of all government expenses for four years
- official status for both English and French
- fair treaties between the government and Native groups in the region
- fair representation in the Canadian Parliament
- respect for existing privileges and customs.

Scene 4: Setting Up a Provisional Government

The Métis had prevented Canada from taking over the North West, and they had shown the Hudson's Bay Company that it no longer ruled the region. Now, who would make laws and keep order? Riel set up a meeting with both the English and French at Red River, and asked them to consider a List of Rights for the region—the conditions under which they would enter Canada's Confederation.

With the List of Rights in hand, Riel was ready to declare a **provisional government** for the region. Though sympathetic to Riel's ideas, the English refused to join him—they did not want to be seen as traitors to the British Crown. Even some of the Métis were uncertain. Finally, Riel and his followers declared their own provisional government. They continued working hard to get the English to support their government. Several meetings later, both the English and the French of Red River agreed on a provisional government—a move that was denounced by the Canadians who lived in the settlement.

Louis Riel and the provisional government of Red River, 1869

Father of Manitoba
Louis Riel

Louis Riel
Born: October 22, 1844, in Red River
Died: Executed on November 16, 1885, in Regina

Early Life:

Riel grew up in the Métis community at Red River. At the age of 13, he was sent to Canada East to study at the College of Montreal. At 19, he left school and worked as a clerk in a law office and became deeply involved in political discussions about the place of the French and Catholic in a confederation with the other colonies. Riel fell in love with a girl in Quebec, Marie Guernon, but her parents branded him as unsuitable because of his Métis and western heritage. In 1869, Riel returned to Red River.

At Red River:

As leader of the Métis, Riel defended their rights when Canada tried to take over Métis land in 1869. With other Métis and Red River residents, he composed the List of Rights that spelled out their conditions for union with Canada. Accused of executing Thomas Scott, a Canadian who lived at Red River, Riel fled to the U.S. just weeks after Manitoba joined Confederation in 1870. He returned to Red River in 1873 and was elected to the Canadian Parliament. Riel was pardoned for the execution of Scott in 1875, provided that he stay out of Canada for five years.

Later Life:

Riel returned to Canada in 1885 to help the Métis living along the North Saskatchewan River defend their rights and their land against new settlers sent West by the Canadian government. The Métis ended up declaring a provisional government and battling Canadian troops. Riel was captured, tried for treason, and executed.

Accomplishments:

As the defender of the rights of the Métis, Riel made it impossible for the Canadian government to ignore the residents of the North West and their demand for land and rights. He is considered by many to be the Father of Manitoba.

Infamous as "The Shot that Set the West Ablaze," this illustration of the execution of Thomas Scott set English Canadians, especially in Ontario, against the Métis and Riel.

PUBLIC MEETING

To AFFORD LOYAL PEOPLE an opportunity of expressing their deep indignation at the vile crimes committed in Rupert's Land, by imprisoning and murdering British and Canadian subjects.

The honour of England was never outraged with impunity, and never will be. Let Canada not be degraded, the honour of the country must be maintained, the blood of the Martyred Scott must not cry in vain for vengeance.

Posted in a small village in eastern Ontario, 1870

Scene 5: The Death of Thomas Scott

Through all the meetings in Red River, a small group of Canadians had shouted insults at the Métis, the French, and the Catholics. The provisional government decided to lock up some of the men to ensure that violence did not break out. One Canadian imprisoned in Fort Garry was Thomas Scott, a violent-tempered man who had attacked one of the Métis with an axe. For weeks, Scott hurled vile insults and threatened to shoot Riel. Finally, the Métis charged Scott with treason and put him on trial. The verdict was guilty. The punishment was death. Thomas Scott was shot on March 4, 1870. To the Métis, the action was just: Scott had challenged their provisional government and uttered threats.

The English residents of Red River were not happy. But the strongest reaction came from the Orangemen of Ontario, a Protestant group with strong anti-Catholic, anti-French views. The Orangemen demanded that the Canadian government send military troops to punish the men responsible for Scott's death.

Scene 6: Terms of Acceptance

In the middle of all the drama at Red River, three negotiators, led by Father Noel Ritchot, headed for Ottawa. They met quietly with John A. Macdonald and his ally, George-Étienne Cartier. Macdonald thought he could outmanoeuvre the westerners. He was wrong. Ritchot continued to insist that the people of the Red River region be treated as equals to any other Canadian citizens. Macdonald finally agreed to all the negotiators' terms. On May 12, 1870, the Province of Manitoba was born.

Manitoba Act

```
20          Cap. 3.          Manitoba.          33 VICT.

                    CAP. III.

An Act to amend and continue the Act 32 and 33 Victoria,
  chapter 3; and to establish and provide for the Govern-
  ment of the Province of Manitoba.

                [Assented to 12th May, 1870.]

Preamble    WHEREAS it is probable that Her Majesty The Queen may,
            pursuant to the British North America Act, 1867, be
pleased to admit Rupert's Land and the North-Western Territory
into the Union or Dominion of Canada, before the next Session of
the Parliament of Canada:

            And Whereas it is expedient to prepare for the transfer of the
said Territories to the Government of Canada at the time ap-
pointed by the Queen for such admission:

            And Whereas it is expedient also to provide for the organiza-
tion of part of the said Territories as a Province, and for the
establishment of a Government therefor, and to make provision
for the Civil Government of the remaining part of the said
Territories, not included within the limits of the Province:

            Therefore Her Majesty, by and with the advice and consent of
the Senate and House of Commons of Canada, enacts as follows:

Province to   1. On, from and after the day upon which the Queen, by and
be formed     with the advice and consent of Her Majesty's Most Honorable
out of N.W.   Privy Council, under the authority of the 146th Section of the
territory     British North America Act, 1867, shall, by Order in Council in
when united   that behalf, admit Rupert's Land and the North-Western Territory
to Canada.    into the Union or Dominion of Canada, there shall be formed out
              of the same a Province, which shall be one of the Provinces of the
Its name and  Dominion of Canada, and which shall be called the Province of
boundaries.   Manitoba, and be bounded as follows: that is to say, commencing
at the point where the meridian of ninety-six degrees west longi-
tude from Greenwich intersects the parallel of forty-nine degrees
north latitude,—thence due west along the said parallel of forty-nine
degrees north latitude (which forms a portion of the boundary line
between the United States of America and the said North-Western
Territory) to the meridian of ninety-nine degrees of west longitude,
—thence due north along the said meridian of ninety-nine degrees
west longitude, to the intersection of the same with the parallel
of fifty degrees and thirty minutes north latitude,—thence due
east along the said parallel of fifty degrees and thirty minutes
north latitude to its intersection with the before-mentioned
meridian of ninety-six degrees west longitude,—thence due south
along the said meridian of ninety-six degrees west longitude to
the place of beginning."
                                                          2.
```

Terms of the Manitoba Bill:

- The new province of Manitoba will be 20 000 square kilometres in size.
- It will be headed by a lieutenant governor, appointed by Canada.
- It will have a nominated (appointed) Upper House of seven members.
- It will have an elected assembly of 24 members.
- It will have two senators in the Canadian Senate and four elected members in the House of Commons. The numbers will increase as the population increases.
- French and English will have equal status.
- The right to **denominational schools** (Catholic and Protestant) is guaranteed.
- 1.4 million acres (567 000 hectares) will be reserved for the Métis residents of the region.
- Canada will pay the new province $27.27 per person, plus an annual subsidy, until the population reaches 400 000.

Telling Their Stories

FATHER NOEL RITCHOT

Watch *Canada: A People's History*, Episode 9: "From Sea to Sea" (16:29:54 to 16:32:16). List three adjectives that describe Father Ritchot, then write a paragraph describing why you think he was successful in securing rights for the people of the new province of Manitoba. Support your opinions with details from this book or from the video clip.

Wolseley—The Soldier.
Colonel Wolseley was one of Britain's most famous military men when Prime Minister Macdonald sent him to Red River in 1869. This sketch shows Wolseley leading a British charge in Egypt in 1882.

Scene 7: Back at Red River

Prime Minister Macdonald sent 1200 soldiers to Red River, under the command of Colonel Garnet Wolseley. Wolseley's instructions were to ensure a peaceful transition to a new government. His British soldiers followed the rules, but the soldiers from Ontario had one simple mission: to hunt down the Métis they thought were responsible for Thomas Scott's death.

They went looking for Riel, but he slipped out of Fort Garry, leaving his breakfast unfinished. They turned on Elzear Goulet, who had served on Scott's jury, and chased him to his death in the freezing river. They drank and brawled, and threatened any Métis they could find.

Scene 8: The New Manitoba

In March 1871, elected members of the new Manitoba legislature and appointed members of the Senate marched behind a ceremonial guard of 100 men from the Ontario Rifles to a private house, the only building big enough to hold them all. The first session of the Manitoba legislature had begun.

In the fall, a group of Fenians—Irish Americans who wanted to overthrow British rule—threatened to invade Manitoba. Their leader thought the Métis might help. Instead, the Métis, with Riel among them, agreed to take up arms to defend the new Canadian province.

That same year, the surveyors returned to Manitoba. This time, they respected the boundaries of the river lots owned by the Métis, but divided all the rest of the tiny province into one-mile square sections. Some sections were reserved for Métis, for schools, and for the Hudson's Bay Company. Almost half of every section, however, was set aside for homesteaders—the families who were already flocking to Canada's newest province.

Winnipeg, 1871

◀ Playback ▶

1. **Who were the main players in the drama at Red River? What did each group want?**

2. **Why did Prime Minister Macdonald decide not to appoint a government at Red River?**

3. **Why were many people at Red River against the actions of the Canadian government?**

4. **Why did the provisional government execute Thomas Scott?**

5. **What rights did the Red River negotiators get for their new province of Manitoba?**

The Back Story

Each group involved in the conflict at Red River thought it was right. The Métis wanted to protect their land rights. The Canadian government wanted to control the North West. The Canadians from Ontario, who were English and Protestant, wanted to keep the Métis, who were French and Catholic, from holding the power in the region.

The Goal

As a class, re-create the drama at Red River. Acting as members of the various sides in the conflict, show how each group was convinced that it was right and everyone else was wrong.

The Steps

1. Separate into three groups, representing the Métis, the Canadian settlers at Red River, and the government of Canada.
2. Review information in the chapter about the beliefs and actions of your group at the time that Manitoba was created. You may also search on the Internet for more information.
3. Each group should choose members to take the role of central characters, such as Prime Minister Macdonald, Louis Riel, and Thomas Scott. Each character delivers an opening statement about whether Thomas Scott should be executed or not.
4. After the opening statements have been delivered, other members of the group should prepare speeches and arguments to present.
5. When all the opening statements and speeches have been presented, debate the issue informally, remaining in role.
6. Each of the principal characters should deliver a final statement. Then, as a class, vote on the issue of Scott's execution. Vote according to your own beliefs, rather than as your character.

Evaluating Your Work

As you work, keep these criteria in mind. Be sure to:
- include additional research about the events at Red River
- prepare opening statements and speeches that are short but well written
- deliver your remarks in a clear voice
- listen attentively while others are speaking
- join the debate by adding opinions, questions, and insights
- vote according to your thoughts and conscience.

History in Action

Dramatizing the Events at Red River

CHAPTER 2

BRITISH COLUMBIA

Hundreds of men poured off the wooden sidewheel steamer that tied up to the dock at the fur-trading post of Fort Victoria on Vancouver Island. They overwhelmed the town, setting up their tents beside the few muddy streets and buying out all the provisions.

Then they were off again, by canoe and boat, headed for the mainland. "Gold!" was their rallying cry, for they all sought their fortunes from the gold that had been found in the sandbars of the Fraser River.

The British possessions on the northwest coast of North America would never be the same again. Little more than one decade later, life between the Rocky Mountains and the Pacific Ocean had dramatically changed.

"A quiet village of about 800 inhabitants. No noise, no bustle, no gamblers, no speculators or interested parties to preach up this or underrate that. A few quiet, gentlemanly-behaved inhabitants, chiefly Scotsmen, secluded as it were from the whole world. As to business there was none, the streets were grown over with grass, and there was not even a cart."

— surveyor Albert Waddington
describes Fort Victoria early in 1858

In 1842, James Douglas chose Victoria for the new western headquarters of the Hudson's Bay Company.

BRITISH COLUMBIA IN 1857

"The place itself appears a perfect Eden in the midst of the dreary wilderness of the Northwest Coast, and so different in its general aspect from the wooded, rugged regions around, that one might be dropped from the clouds into its present position."

— JAMES DOUGLAS DESCRIBING SOUTHERN
VANCOUVER ISLAND IN 1843

On a spring day in 1842, James Douglas and a band of men from the Hudson's Bay Company sailed into a pretty harbour on the southern end of Vancouver Island. They were looking for new headquarters for the fur-trading company. A year later, a company fort had been built. Fort Victoria became the western headquarters of the Hudson's Bay Company.

By 1857, the company was firmly established, with Douglas overseeing the vast territory to the east and north. On the west, this land was bounded by the Pacific Ocean, with Vancouver Island and the Queen Charlotte Islands lying along the coastal shore. Far to the east, beyond tangled chains of mountains, lay the Rocky Mountains.

To the north—well, who knew exactly what lay to the north? Though fur-trading posts existed and white explorers had followed the courses of several rivers and Native trails from the interior to the sea, there was no clear map of this vast territory that the Hudson's Bay Company had named New Caledonia.

THE NATIVE PEOPLE

The British Columbia of the 1850s was home to about 75 000 Native people. Most lived along the coast, fishing and hunting game. Other Native nations ranged over the interior of the region, following the salmon when they came far upstream to spawn and hunting deer, moose, and other animals.

Native village on B.C. coast

THE NEWCOMERS

Fewer than a thousand people lived in this vast territory, most around Fort Victoria where they worked for the Hudson's Bay Company. Some were independent settlers who farmed or ran small sawmills. Some were sailors.

A hundred or so people lived at Nanaimo, where the Hudson's Bay Company had built a small fort. Fort Langley, in the wide valley of the Fraser River, was the largest fur-trading post on the mainland. The fur brigades came to the fort, by canoe, on horseback, and on foot, bringing the thick furs trapped in the lands to the north. Dotting this north country were half a dozen fur posts, the first settlements of the newcomers to New Caledonia.

Fort at Nanaimo, 1850s

Barkerville was the biggest and the busiest of the gold rush towns.

Reverend James Reynard, an English missionary, arrived in Barkerville in 1868. In a town that was often too rough to welcome preachers, he established St. Saviour's Church, one of the first permanent churches in the area.

GOLD RUSH: WINNERS AND LOSERS

The rumour spread from the Fraser River to Fort Victoria to the Columbia River to San Francisco. Gold had been found in New Caledonia.

Early in 1858, Fort Victoria was suddenly overrun by thousands of people, filled with dreams of finding gold along the Fraser River. Altogether, about 30 000 people arrived. That summer, they panned for gold on the sandbars of the Fraser River and headed north on rough Native and fur-trade trails. Few dreams came true. By fall, many of them had returned home.

The next year and the next, thousands more arrived. Prospectors found deposits of gold in the **Cariboo**, about 500 kilometres from the coast. There, on Williams Creek and a dozen other small creeks, they built towns. Some stayed for years, while others went back home, broke and disappointed.

BARKERVILLE: BOOM TOWN

Thousands of people flocked to the Cariboo between 1860 and 1870 to prospect for gold, to mine, to set up businesses, or to work at anything that was available. The biggest of the gold rush towns was Barkerville.

During its days as a boom town, Barkerville attracted people from around the world. Wellington Delaney Moses led a group of Black people from California to Victoria in 1858. In 1862, he took his "hair invigorator" and barbering skills to Barkerville, where he operated "fashion saloons," cutting hair and selling ribbons and silks. Loo Chuck Fan and Loo Choo Fan were partners in the Kwong Lee Company store. They sold groceries and provisions—rice, tea, sugar, tobacco, clothes, boots, hardware, and mining tools. Harry Jones came to Barkerville with the Welsh Adventurers, a group of Welsh miners who decided to try their luck in the Cariboo. He represented the region in the B.C. legislature from 1903 to 1909.

GOLD RUSH WOMEN

Thousands of men poured into B.C. to mine for gold. Very few women arrived at the same time. Men with plans to stay wanted wives. In September 1862, 62 English women arrived at Victoria harbour. All businesses closed for the day, and eager young men rowed out to be the first to see them.

Groups of women were brought to the Cariboo to work as dance partners for the miners. They became known as Hurdy Gurdy Girls. A few women opened businesses. Jenny Allen came to Barkerville in 1862. She ran a boarding house for miners and nursed them through injuries and illnesses. Later, she moved up to operating hotels and saloons. Jenny died in 1870 when her carriage tumbled into a canyon. "All the flags in Barkerville were hung at half-mast," reported the newspaper, "... she dressed like a man, drank like a man and died like a man."

Catherine Schubert was the only woman in a group of 200 gold seekers who travelled overland from Red River to the Cariboo in 1862. The journey took five months, and for most of the way, Catherine walked with her three young children. Her fourth child was born before she reached the goldfields.

◀ Playback ▶

1. Describe life in British Columbia before the gold rush.

2. What effects did the gold rush have on British Columbia?

3. Why did so many people flock to the region when they heard news of the discovery of gold? If you had lived at that time, would you have come to seek gold? Why or why not?

THE NEW COLONY

The great numbers of people invading his territory worried Governor James Douglas. Would the Americans look on this as a chance to take over? Would prospectors and those who came with them fight, kill, and steal from the settlers and Native people? The British government heeded Douglas's warnings and created the new mainland colony of British Columbia. The two colonies of British Columbia and Vancouver Island were then combined to create one colony, with Douglas as governor.

James Douglas: Old Square Toes

James Douglas
Born: British Guyana, 1803
Died: Victoria, 1877

Early Life:

Educated in Scotland, Douglas was apprenticed to the North West Company at age 16. In 1825, he took up a post with the Hudson's Bay Company at Fort St. James in New Caledonia. He married Amelia Connolly, daughter of a fur trader and his Cree wife. Douglas moved to Fort Vancouver and then on to Fort Victoria in 1842.

Life at Victoria:

Douglas was named chief factor at Fort Victoria in 1849, and appointed governor of the colony of Vancouver Island in 1851. When the gold rush hit in 1858, Douglas made sure British rule extended to the mainland. For his efforts, he was appointed governor of mainland British Columbia as well. Douglas oversaw the building of the Cariboo Road, and made treaties with Native people. His stern appearance and manner won him the nickname "Old Square Toes."

Accomplishments:

Douglas secured B.C. for Britain, built the Cariboo Road, and established a justice system in the region.

The Cariboo Road solved the problem of getting miners and supplies in and sending gold out of the Cariboo mining area. Parts of the 650-kilometre road had to be blasted out of solid rock.

THE CARIBOO ROAD

Governor James Douglas faced an immediate problem: How would the gold miners get to the Cariboo? How would the gold make its way back to Victoria? How would stores in the mining towns get their goods? Douglas decided to build a wagon road to the Cariboo. The Royal Engineers, who had been sent to the colony to build roads, and private contractors built the Cariboo Road from Fort Yale on the Fraser River to Barkerville. The Cariboo Road opened up the interior of British Columbia.

Chinese Miners

Many Chinese came from California to try their luck in British Columbia's gold rush.

"This much-enduring and industrious race are generally to be found in little clusters, at work upon the diggings deserted by the whites ... and will doubtless at the end of the year, by means of their frugality, save more than their white brother is likely to, in spite of his higher gains ... It is the fashion on the Pacific coast to abuse and ill-treat the Chinaman in every possible way; and I really must tell my friends ... they are hard-working, sober, and law-abiding—three scarce qualities among people in the station."

— Miner Byron Johnson, travelling in the Cariboo in the early 1860s

THE WORLD OF NATIVE NATIONS

A Haida potlatch.
Smallpox killed
thousands of Haida
in the 1860s.

The man, just one among thousands who disembarked from a ship in Victoria harbour, was feeling unwell. As he wandered around the port, he came into contact with many others, including some of the Native people who camped near the fort. Soon after, they were seized by fever and aching bones; rashes and blisters broke out on their bodies.

Smallpox had arrived in British Columbia again, after epidemics in 1782 and 1836. People of European background had some defences, but the Native people had no immunity to it. The smallpox began to spread among the Native people living near the fort. Governor Douglas ordered them to return to their villages along the coast. Wherever they went, they spread the disease.

In one year, at least one-third of the Native people in the region died. Some groups, especially those on the coast who lived close together in villages, were hit especially hard. Before the smallpox epidemic, there were 8000 Haida living on the Queen Charlotte Islands. A year later, there were 800.

The 1860s brought more than smallpox to the Native people. Settlers were arriving. As the newcomers moved into the region, they took over land that the Native nations considered their own. Though people like James Douglas wanted to make sure that Native people had land, others were less generous.

The Native people of British Columbia did not give up their land; they did not sign treaties with the new government. A hundred and fifty years later, they are still battling to regain their land.

The Chilcotin War

How to get to the goldfields? Whichever way a miner looked, mountains, cliffs, rushing rivers, canyons, bogs, and long distances made the journey difficult.

In 1864, immigrant Alfred Waddington looked at the way Bute Inlet cut inland towards the Chilcotin River and wondered if a road could be built along a Chilcotin route.

Waddington sent in surveyors, who mistreated the Tsilhqot'in people they met along the way. The surveyors insisted on their right to survey a road that would cut across land that the Tsilhqot'in considered to be their own. Did the Native people also fear that the newcomers brought smallpox? Whatever the reason, some of the surveyors were killed by the Tsilhqot'in. When the news reached the government, men were sent out to arrest the Tsilhqot'in who were responsible for the deaths. They were put on trial, and five were executed.

No road was built. To this day, the Tsilhqot'in are among the fiercest resisters of any attempts to take over what they consider their territory.

> "*Shall we allow a few vagrants to prevent forever industrious*
> *settlers from settling on unoccupied lands? Not at all ...*
> *Locate reservations for them on which to earn their own living,*
> *and if they trespass on white settlers, punish them severely.*"
> — Amor de Cosmos

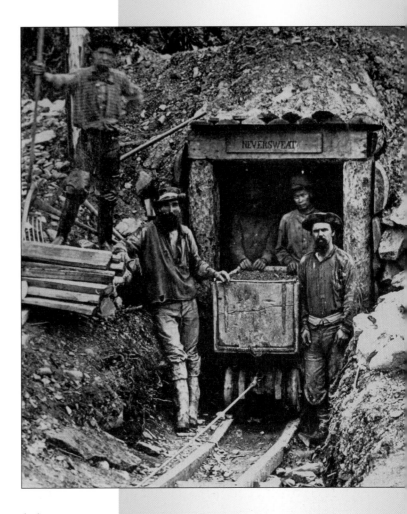

The Neversweat mine in the Cariboo goldfields

Barkerville
Quesnel

Nootka Sound

Nanaimo

Victoria New Westminster

Gold rush towns, like Barkerville, sprang up almost overnight in the Cariboo region of New Caledonia. They disappeared almost as quickly when the gold ran out. From "the gold capital of the world" in 1858, Barkerville had become just another abandoned mining town by 1900.

BRITISH COLUMBIA IN 1867

By 1867, many of the gold rushers had left British Columbia. The number of Native people had shrunk to about 30 000. The number of newcomers from around the world had grown to about 10 000. Most of these new-comers were from Britain, Europe, the United States, and Canada. About 1600 were from China.

New towns had replaced the fur-trading forts as the main centres of settlement. New roads and trails connected the towns. Their streets were lined with stores, hotels, restaurants, schools, and churches. British Columbia was growing.

In Debt

There was a cost to the growth of British Columbia. The colony was building roads, as well as paying for a government, for police, and for judges—most of it on borrowed money. How could British Columbia deal with its debt? Could it continue to exist?

British Columbia had three options. It could remain a British colony. It could join Canada. It could join the United States. Some people suggested that the colony could become an independent country, but few supported that position. No one was sure which option was better for British Columbia—or, rather, everyone was sure, but few agreed.

Debating the Future
What were the arguments for the choice that British Columbia had to make?

1. Remain a British Colony

FOR

British Columbia is a lot like Britain. Many people here are from Britain, belong to the Church of England, know British customs, and enjoy a British lifestyle. The British Navy, stationed nearby, can defend the colony against American attempts to take it over.

AGAINST

Britain doesn't want to keep British Columbia as a colony. The colony is far away, and supporting it is expensive. Many people living here are from Canada, the United States, Europe, and China, and we are tired of the way British people try to dominate life in the colony.

2. Join the United States

FOR

In 1867, the United States bought Alaska from the Russians. Now British Columbia has American neighbours to the north and American neighbours to the south. For trade and immigration, it makes sense to have one territory running from north to south. The U.S. is powerful in the region, and it would probably be easier to join the U.S. than to fight against it. Many Americans live here now.

AGAINST

The U.S. is not British. Our traditions, laws, and many of the people living here are of British origin. British Columbia will be lost in such a big country, and we will be ignored.

3. Join Canada

FOR

Canada is a new, exciting nation. We no longer want to be a British colony, and we don't want to be ruled by the United States. If we join Canada, we can elect a government instead of having one chosen for us. All the land from Ontario to the Rocky Mountains belongs to Canada, and adding British Columbia makes a nation that stretches from sea to sea.

AGAINST

The rest of Canada is far away. The people in the rest of Canada outnumber us. We might be ignored if we join this country. How could we get what we need and want?

JOINING CANADA

Britain didn't seem to care about its Pacific colony. In fact, it told the B.C. government that the colony should join Canada. Few people wanted to join the U.S., and if British Columbia remained independent, it would probably be swallowed by the U.S. Joining Canada seemed to be the best idea—if the colony could obtain good terms. British Columbia wanted Canada to pay its huge debt and build a wagon road—or even a railway—from the rest of Canada to the coast.

Delegates went to Ottawa to lay out the colony's terms for union. They were greeted with great friendship. Yes, Canada would pay the colony's debt. Most surprisingly, Canada promised to begin building a railway to the west coast within two years. The terms for Confederation were much better than the delegates had dared hope for.

Some members of the Canadian Parliament were horrified at the promises, and threatened to vote against them. But Sir George-Étienne Cartier fought for British Columbia and won. On July 20, 1871, British Columbia became a new province in Canada.

Amor de Cosmos

Amor de Cosmos
Born: William Smith, Nova Scotia, 1825
Died: Victoria, 1897

Early Life:

Born in Nova Scotia, William Smith went to California at the age of 26, where he worked as a photographer and speculated in real estate. Finding it difficult to get his mail with so many Smiths in the area, in 1854 he changed his name to Amor de Cosmos, "lover of the world."

In British Columbia:

Amor de Cosmos moved to Victoria in 1858 with the first wave of gold rush prospectors from California. He founded a newspaper, the *British Colonist*, to promote political discussion and reform. As the newspaper's editor, he criticized James Douglas for being undemocratic. He also advocated the union of all British colonies in North America. He was elected to the B.C. legislative assembly in 1863. In 1871, he was elected to federal Parliament. He returned to B.C. and served as the province's premier from 1872 to 1874, when he was elected again to Parliament.

Later Life:

Amor de Cosmos's views became increasingly racist. He retired after losing his seat in Parliament. Always considered an eccentric, he was declared incompetent to manage his own affairs in 1895.

Accomplishments:

De Cosmos fought to unite Vancouver Island and the mainland. He battled for B.C. to become part of Canada.

REGRETS

People who loved Britain complained about the union. "Society in B.C. is greatly changed for the worse," sniffed one. The new government, said another, contained "not one of whom you would care to have for a friend, or to ask to your house." Happier were the majority of people who supported union with Canada. At midnight on July 19, 1871, bells rang, guns were fired, and fireworks soared into the night. Amor de Cosmos was elected as a member of Parliament in Ottawa.

Eight years later, people were not so happy. Not one metre of rails had been laid. Angry and frustrated, British Columbians petitioned the British government for help. In Parliament, Amor de Cosmos stood up to introduce a resolution calling for British Columbia to **secede** from the union. No one supported his motion, and it disappeared. But it would not be the last time that British Columbians would be unhappy with the government in Ottawa.

New Westminster had always celebrated May Day, the Queen's birthday, but the owner of this hotel thought he could sell more food and drink on Dominion Day. He claimed these Dominion Day celebrations in 1878 were the first ever held in the town.

◄ Playback ►

1. **What happened to the First Nations in British Columbia during and after the gold rush?**

2. **In the North West, on the other side of the Rockies, Canadian government representatives signed treaties with many First Nations. Why did they not sign treaties in British Columbia?**

3. **What were British Columbia's choices after the gold rush? Why did it decide to join Canada?**

The Back Story

In 1871, British Columbia chose to become part of Canada. That choice was one of three that the colony had, and not everyone was happy with the final decision.

The Goal

In a small group, create a newspaper for the day that British Columbia joins Confederation.

The Steps

1. With your group, decide on the features you plan to include in your newspaper. Your newspaper should include several news stories (people's reactions, the Native point of view, excitement about the railway, and so on), an editorial, and a letter to the editor that shows an opinion different from the editorial. You can include any other items you wish.

2. Divide the work among your group members. You may want to assign an editor, writers, designers, and artists.

3. Research information for your articles using this book and other sources.

4. Complete your articles, then have group members peer-edit them.

5. As a group, decide on the visuals, layout, and design for your newspaper.

6. Prepare your final, designed newspaper. Display it with others created by your classmates, or explain it orally to the class.

Evaluating Your Work

As you work, keep these criteria in mind. Be sure to:
- base your work on historical fact
- show various points of view about the topic
- include a variety of types of articles
- be persuasive or objective where necessary
- write clearly and use correct grammar, spelling, and punctuation
- use an attractive design and layout.

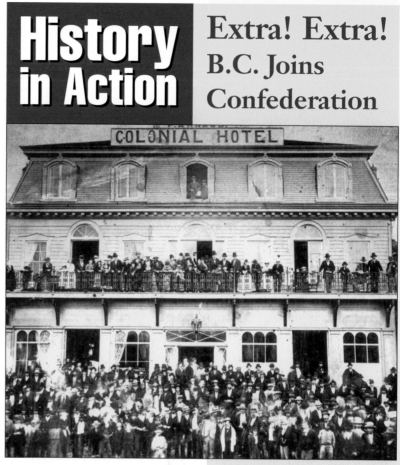

History in Action

Extra! Extra!
B.C. Joins Confederation

COLONIAL HOTEL

CHAPTER 3

ON THE PRAIRIES

Little changed on the day in 1869 when Canada took possession of the North West. Thousands of kilometres away from Ottawa and sparsely populated, the North West meant little to the average Canadian—and Canada meant little to the residents of the North West.

No one was sure just how many people lived in this vast region. Estimates said that the territory was home to 25 000 to 35 000 Native people—the Assiniboine and Blackfoot along the American border and the Cree to the north and east.

Probably about 10 000 Métis, descendants of Native mothers and French or British fur traders, also lived in the North West. Most lived at Red River, while others lived farther west, along the North Saskatchewan River.

Métis and Native families meet on the empty prairie near present-day Calgary. The Métis invented the Red River cart for travelling long distances, especially on their annual buffalo hunts. The cart, including its wheels, was made entirely of wood, which made it easy to repair.

Perhaps 2000 white people lived in the territory, a number that was rapidly increasing in the Red River area. Beyond Red River was a scattering of traders, mostly at Hudson's Bay posts, and missionaries hoping to convert Native people to Christianity.

The Manitou Stone

The immensely heavy stone was like no other rock in the land that is now Alberta. Native legend said it came to Earth in a blazing fireball—a meteorite sent from the sky to protect the Blackfoot and the Cree in whose land it lay. For centuries, people came to touch and take strength from Nitawh-Sinanni, the Manitou Stone. If it was ever removed, the legend said, then disease, famine, and war would come upon the land.

Parson John—Methodist missionary John McDougall—hated the Native spiritual beliefs and traditions; he wanted the Native people to embrace his Christian god instead. If he removed the stone, he would show the superiority of his religion. If nothing evil happened, he could say that the white man's god had triumphed over traditional beliefs.

In the fall of 1868, as the prairie turned golden with frost, Parson John and a team of men took a block and tackle to the spot where Nitawh-Sinanni stood. They removed the sacred stone and hauled it to the front yard of the mission house.

From the Sources

"[The next year] brought all the three evils upon the Indians; and never, probably, since the first trader had reached the country had so many afflictions of war, famine, and plague fallen upon the Crees and the Blackfoot as during the year which succeeded the useless removal of their Manito-stone from the lone hill-top upon which the skies had cast it."

— William Francis Butler, who was travelling through the West for the Manitoba government after Parson John removed the sacred stone

DISEASE: THE SCOURGE OF SMALLPOX

Smallpox first arrived on the plains in 1781. No one knows the number of Native people who died. The scourge came again in the 1820s and the 1830s. In 1869, smallpox spread from infected men on a boat that ran the river south from Fort Benton in the Montana Territory to the Native people on the plains. Before long, it was running rampant among the Blackfoot and the Cree.

A missionary who travelled the region at the time estimated that 2500 Cree—almost one in three—and as many Blackfoot were killed by smallpox in 1869–1870. The whites in the region were not all spared: the three sisters of John McDougall, the missionary who stole the sacred stone, died in the epidemic.

FAMINE: THE END OF THE BUFFALO

For centuries, millions of shaggy-headed buffalo roamed the prairies, grazing north and south with the seasons. With them went the Native people, hunting buffalo for food, for robes to keep them warm, and for the sinews they used for their bows. As the Métis population grew larger, they also relied on the buffalo. The annual buffalo hunt, with carts heading west from Red River over hundreds of kilometres of the plains, was the key event of Métis life, providing pemmican for food and for trading with the fur traders.

By the 1870s, thanks to repeating rifles, the buffalo became easy prey. Hundreds of thousands were slaughtered mainly for their hides, which were turned into inexpensive leather. Plagues of grasshoppers ate the prairie to bare dirt, driving many of the remaining buffalo south across the American border. There, the herds were also killed for food and hides. White hunting parties shot buffalo for sport.

The disappearance of the buffalo meant starvation for many Native people

> "The buffalo ... is rapidly disappearing; year by year, the prairies, which once shook beneath the tread of countless herds of bison, are becoming denuded of animal life, and year by year the affliction of starvation comes with an ever-increasing intensity upon the land ... during the present winter, I have traversed the plains from the Red River to the Rocky Mountains without seeing even one solitary animal upon 1200 miles of prairie."
>
> — W.F. Butler, in his report on the North West in 1871

As the buffalo were slaughtered, their bones piled up on the prairies. First Nations and Métis people collected the bones and delivered them to train depots, where they were shipped to factories in eastern Canada and ground into fertilizer. Collectors were paid five cents for a ton of buffalo bones.

and Métis. The Blackfoot, in what would become Alberta, were "selling their horses for a mere song, eating gophers, mice, and for the first time have hunted the Antelope and nearly killed them all off ... Strong young men were now so weak that some of them could hardly walk. Others who last winter were fat and hearty are mere skin and bone."

WAR: BLACKFOOT VS CREE

As the buffalo disappeared, Native groups were forced to travel outside their traditional territories in order to find food. The Cree wandered west, following the remaining buffalo herds. They entered the territory of the Blackfoot and the Assiniboine, their traditional enemies.

For five years in the 1860s, great battles took place between Native nations. Hundreds were killed, both the young men who fought the battles and the older men and women and children who were attacked in their camps.

In 1870, Cree met Blackfoot near the junction of the Oldman and St. Mary's Rivers, in present-day southern Alberta. Counterattack followed attack. The Blackfoot owned the better weapons. More than 200 Cree and 40 Blackfoot were killed.

This was the last battle of the plains war. The following year, the Cree and Blackfoot chiefs concluded a peace agreement.

Blackfoot and Cree chiefs negotiated a peace treaty in 1871 that ended years of war between the two great nations.

OVER THE BORDER

Just three years before Canada took over the North West, people began to stream into the Montana Territory, south of the American border. They were looking for gold. In just a few months, fighting, drinking, and killing transformed the territory into the worst example of the lawless West.

The newcomers pushed the Native people who lived in the territory, and they pushed back. Soldiers sent to suppress them built 33 military posts and forts south of the border. The Americans decided to starve the Native people by killing the buffalo. In three years, about 3.5 million buffalo were slaughtered on the American plains—some by soldiers, some by hunters, some for food, and some for sport. The Native people killed fewer than 150 000.

**American settlers
heading to the prairies**

> *"The whisky brought among
> us by the traders is fast
> killing us off. We are
> powerless before this evil.
> We are unable to resist the
> temptation to drink when
> brought in contact with the
> white man's water.
> Our horses, buffalo robes,
> and other articles of trade
> go for whisky."*
>
> — CHIEF CROWFOOT

THE WHISKY FORTS

The traders headed north on the Whoop-Up Trail, with
yokes of oxen, teams in a convoy, dragging wagons through
deep and muddy ruts. In the wagons were the supplies and
goods the traders needed to keep themselves going. The
most important cargo, though, was the whisky that they
would trade to the Native people north of the border in
return for fine furs from the northern territory.

The Native people had no experience with alcohol
before the first traders arrived. It made them drunk and
addicted. From the time the first trader offered whisky,
many Native trappers wanted only alcohol for their furs.

Honest traders refused to trade in alcohol. But traders
who invaded the Montana Territory were determined to
make their fortunes any way they could. The competition
in Montana was stiff, and there were few traders on the
Canadian side of the line. So Montana men began to build
their whisky forts on the north side of the border. They
diluted their whisky with water and added ginger, paint,

and even oil to give the alcohol a fiery taste. The whisky forts attracted large numbers of Native people who wanted to trade for "firewater"—and who sometimes stole the traders' horses instead.

MASSACRE AT CYPRESS HILLS

Among the American traders were "wolfers," men who killed wolves with poisoned bait and collected a bounty for each animal. Their poison also killed dogs that belonged to the Native people. The wolfers were considered the lowest of the traders—violent, dishonest, and often drunk.

Thirteen wolfers came to the Cypress Hills in May 1873. They were angry and frustrated. A few days before, a group of Cree had stolen 40 of their horses. When they couldn't find the culprits, the wolfers set out to kill any Native people they could find. In the hills near a whisky fort, they found a group of Assiniboine. Fearing trouble, their chief urged his people to leave, but the younger men refused.

The wolfers advanced. They fired one shot, then another and another. They bombarded the Assiniboine camp with bullets from their repeating rifles. When all the Assinboine were dead or had fled into the bush, the wolfers destroyed the camp.

Some accounts of the attack say that 22 people were killed, while others say that as many as 200 died. Whatever the death toll, the massacre at Cypress Hills took on a symbolic importance, representing all that was negative about American influence.

◄ Playback ►

1. What was Nitawh-Sinanni? What was its importance to the Blackfoot and the Cree? What happened to it?

2. What three tragedies happened to the Native people of the prairies in the 1860s and 1870s? Describe the effects of the tragedies on the Native people.

3. Who traded alcohol to the Native people? What were the effects of the whisky trade?

The North-West Mounted Police chased the whisky traders off the prairies and brought law and order to the West.

"It is quite evident to me ... that the United States will do all they can short of war to get possession of the western territory and that we must take immediate and vigorous steps to counteract them."

— PRIME MINISTER JOHN A. MACDONALD

CANADA: A PEOPLE'S HISTORY, 10: 10:04:44

POLICING THE WEST

Not long after Canada took over the North West in 1869, Prime Minister Macdonald began making plans for policing the huge region. The Americans were spending millions of dollars sending soldiers to fight the Native people in the American midwest. Macdonald had other ideas. He thought that a police force could bring law and order to the North West. The force would protect Native people from whisky traders, keep the area from becoming as violent as the American midwest, and show Americans that Canada was serious about holding the North West.

"As matters at present rest, the region of the Saskatchewan is without law, order, or security for life or property; robbery and murder for years have gone unpunished; Indian massacres are unchecked even in close vicinity of the Hudson Bay Company's posts, and all civil and legal institutions are entirely unknown."

— WILLIAM FRANCIS BUTLER, 1871

THE NORTH-WEST MOUNTED POLICE

In the autumn of 1873, when Macdonald heard news of the Cypress Hills massacre, he ordered the first 150 North-West Mounted Police recruits to head west. They travelled by steamship to the head of the Great Lakes. The recruits disembarked and then set out to conquer the 725 kilometres of rough trail to Fort Garry. Though many had never ridden a horse before, they managed to make it to the fort, where they spent the winter. The next spring, another 150 men arrived, and they began the long march west.

The Long March, 1874

The North-West Mounted Police did not have an easy trip west. Thunder and lightning caused the horses to stampede. The men were short of food and tortured by mosquitoes. Swamps were often the only source of drinking water. Mud and hills taxed the oxen, and long hikes across a prairie exhausted men and horses.

Métis and Native people made such treks easily—they were used to the country. The police recruits were not. Some deserted, but most stayed with the long column of men, horses, oxen, and carts that curled west. After three months, they reached Fort Whoop-Up, ready to chase out the whisky traders. They were too late. All the traders but one had left as soon as they heard the Mounties were coming. The police built their first post nearby, and then spread out to build others.

The law had arrived in the North West.

Many of the recruits with the North-West Mounted Police had never ridden a horse before they started the Long March to the West in 1874.

NWMP HEROES

Within a few years, people in eastern Canada were calling the men of the North-West Mounted Police heroes. Often, one policeman was responsible for a large region. If he was challenged, he could not hope to win with violence. It took courage, respect, and authority to police the West.

Jerry Potts
Born: Fort McKenzie, U.S., 1840
Died: July 14, 1896, Fort Macleod, N.W.T.

Jerry Potts

Early Life:
Jerry Potts's father was a Scotsman; his mother was a member of the Blackfoot Nation. He was a great warrior and hunter with the Blackfoot and worked as a guide and scout for Americans.

Life with the NWMP:
In 1874, Potts joined the North-West Mounted Police as a guide, scout, and interpreter—he spoke English, Cree, Blackfoot, and Crow. He led the NWMP west, and helped find a good site for their first post, Fort Macleod, on an island in the river near Fort Whoop-Up. Potts worked with the NWMP for many years, acting as a diplomat between the police and the Blackfoot.

Accomplishments:
Potts kept relations friendly between the police and the Blackfoot, and helped negotiate Treaty 7, guaranteeing them hunting rights, reserve lands, and supplies. He convinced the Blackfoot not to join in the **Northwest Rebellion** in 1885.

James Macleod

Early Life:
Born in Scotland, James Macleod emigrated with his family to Ontario. After practising law, he joined the Wolseley expedition to Red River in 1870.

Life with the NWMP:
Macleod joined the NWMP as superintendent shortly after the force was formed, and was one of the leaders on the Long March west. He developed a strong friendship with Jerry Potts. Macleod earned a reputation as a fair man who treated Métis and Native people as equals, and as a hard worker, a hard rider, and a good leader.

Accomplishments:
Macleod won the respect and trust of his fellow NWMP, the Métis, and the Native people. He helped negotiate Treaty 7 with the Blackfoot.

James Macleod
Born: Scotland, 1836   Died: Calgary, 1894

THE TREATIES: END OF AN ERA

Whisky, war, disease, and the arrival of new settlers in an old land—the traditional way of life of the Native people could not survive these massive changes in the North West. Eager to open the West to settlement, the Canadian government wanted to avoid trouble with the Native people when the surveyors arrived, followed by settlers ready to build homesteads. It set out to sign treaties with every Native group in the North West.

In the treaties, the First Nations signed away some of their rights to the land they had always occupied. In return, Canada would set aside **reserves** of land where Native people could hunt and fish. They were promised annual payments for each band member, as well as farm implements, fishing nets, clothing, cattle, and food.

The Native people were not convinced that the treaties would protect them. They believed the land belonged to them. But was it possible for them to survive? The buffalo were gone, disease had killed many of them, and settlers were coming.

Across the West, First Nations were faced with the advance of settlers and traders. Signing treaties with the government seemed to be the only way they would survive.

In 1876, the Cree, living in present-day Saskatchewan and Alberta, debated their choices. In the end, the disappearance of the buffalo persuaded them to accept a treaty. They feared they would starve without the Canadian government's help. They signed the treaty, as did other First Nations in the North West. The Native people believed they were signing as equals, and that they were being guaranteed a dignified future. But the Canadian government had already passed the **Indian Act**, which declared that all Native people were wards of the state and that the government had the right to make all decisions for them. Later, when the food and farm tools they had been promised did not arrive, the Native people learned that the treaties did not protect them at all.

From the Sources

"We are brothers ... I see Indians gathering ... I see them receiving money from the Queen's Commissioners to purchase clothing for their children ... At the same time, I see them enjoying their hunting and fishing as before, I see them retaining their old mode of living—with the Queen's gift in addition."

"The whole day was occupied with this discussion on the food question. It was the turning point with regards to the treaty ... They were anxious to learn to support themselves by agriculture ... and they dreaded that during the transition period they would be swept off by disease or famine."

— North West Lieutenant Governor Alexander Morris
(*Canada: A People's History*, 10: 10:23:12; 10:25:34)

◀ Playback ▶

1. **Why did the Canadian government send the North-West Mounted Police to the West?**

2. **What was the purpose of the treaties signed between Native people and the government? What results did the Native people want from the treaties? What did the government want?**

3. **Who was Jerry Potts? What were his accomplishments?**

Telling Their Stories

CROWFOOT

The following quotations tell why many Native people struggled over signing the government's treaties. Watch "Pieces of Pemmican" (10:21:40 to 10:27:07) and "The Land of Discontent" (10:39:36 to 10:47:09) in *Canada: A People's History*, Episode 10, to learn more about this difficult decision.

"White men have already taken the best locations and built houses in any place they please ... American traders and others are forming large settlements on Belly River, the best winter hunting grounds ... We all see the day when the buffalo will be killed and we shall have nothing more to live on. Then you will come to our camps and see the poor Blackfeet starving."

— Crowfoot, chief of the Blackfoot

"The governor mentions how much land is to be given to us. He says 640 acres, one mile square for each family. This is our land! It isn't a piece of pemmican to be cut off and given back to us. It is our land and we will take what we want."

— Poundmaker, a Cree chief opposed to signing a treaty

"Can we stop the power of the white man from spreading over the land like the grasshoppers that cloud the sky and then fall to consume every blade of grass and every leaf of the trees in the path? I think not."

— Star Blanket, an older chief who thinks the Cree have no alternative

"We want none of the Queen's presents. When we set a fox trap, we scatter pieces of meat all round, but when the fox gets into the trap, we knock him on the head. We want no bait."

— Big Bear, Cree chief explaining why he will not sign the treaty

The Back Story

The decision of First Nations to sign treaties with Canadian representatives was both difficult and monumental. Today, many people think that the treaties were unfair and hurt the future of Canada's First Nations. Some believe that the treaties were a difficult but necessary choice.

The Goal

In role as a young Native person at the time of the treaties, write and present a speech either supporting or opposing a treaty with the government of Canada.

The Steps

1. Review the material in the chapter, paying particular attention to the arguments for and against treaties.
2. Complete a brief chart like the one below. Try to consider at least three reasons for each side of the issue.

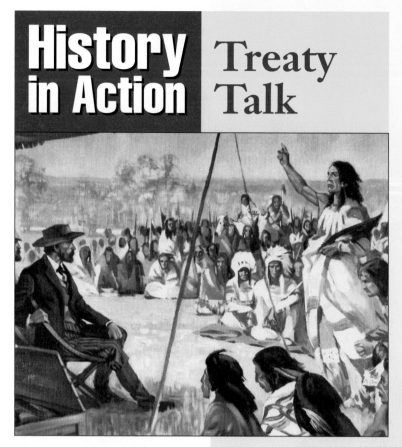

History in Action   Treaty Talk

Arguments in Favour of a Treaty	Arguments Opposed to a Treaty	My Key Concerns/Fears

3. Write a one- to two-page speech to support your opinion on the subject.
4. Deliver your speech to a special tribal council (your classmates) that will be making the final decision to support or reject a treaty. Add any comments or questions as the council discusses the issue.
5. After listening and participating, review your thoughts and cast your final vote. Discuss the results. (Remember it is possible that the debate may change your decision.)

Evaluating Your Work

As you work, keep these criteria in mind. Be sure to:
- include information from the text material and any notes that you have made
- include a pro/con chart to help you clarify your thoughts and ideas
- include a persuasive speech of the proper length
- deliver your speech loudly and clearly to the tribal council
- revisit the issue after listening to the debate and reviewing your ideas.

CHAPTER 4

POLITICS, SETTLEMENT, AND RAILWAYS

Driving the Golden Spike, by Hon. D. A.

I n the decade that followed Confederation in 1867, Canada went from an idea in the heads of politicians to a country that stretched from the Atlantic to the Pacific. By 1873, it included Nova Scotia, New Brunswick, Prince Edward Island, Quebec, Ontario, Manitoba, the North West Territory, and British Columbia. It was home to almost four million Canadians and occupied 8.5 million square kilometres of land.

Promises had been made to the people of British Columbia and to the Métis and Native people in the North West. Many would be delayed or broken as Prime Minister Macdonald became involved in a scandal and then marched ahead with his plans to bring thousands of settlers to the prairies.

Surrounded by railway workers, Donald A. Smith, a director of the Canadian Pacific Railway Company, drove the last spike to complete the CPR on November 7, 1885, in Craigellachie, B.C. The Dominion of Canada had finally fulfilled its promise to the people of British Columbia.

Sir Hugh Allan

Sir George-Étienne Cartier

Sir John A. Macdonald

From the Sources

Dear Sir Hugh:

The friends of the government will expect to be assisted with funds in the pending elections, and any amount which you or your company shall advance for that purpose shall be re-couped to you.

A memorandum of immediate requirements is below.

Very Truly Yours, Geo. E. Cartier

NOW WANTED	
Sir John A. Macdonald	$25,000
Hon. Mr. Langevin	15,000
Sir G.E.C.	20,000
Sir J.A. (Add'l)	10,000
Hon. Mr. Langevin	10,000
Sir G.E.C.	30,000

— letter from George-Étienne Cartier
to Hugh Allan

PROMISES AND SCANDALS

When British Columbia joined Confederation in 1867, Canada promised to start a railway within two years and to complete a transcontinental line by 1877. Could railway builders lay steel rails through rock, muskeg, and chains of mountains? Could this young country afford to build a railway that would be the longest in the world?

If Prime Minister John A. Macdonald and his closest ally, George-Étienne Cartier, had any doubts, they kept them well hidden. The difficult terrain would be conquered. The money would be found. In 1872, when Parliament passed the bill to build the transcontinental railway, Cartier declared: "All aboard for the West!"

The Pacific Scandal

Soon after the bill passed, Macdonald called a national election for October 1872. His Conservative Party won, but it had been a difficult campaign. Macdonald was re-elected, but Cartier lost his seat. Then, a scandal broke. Newspapers reported that the Conservative campaign had been financed by Hugh Allan, a shipping magnate and railway builder from Montreal. What had Allan been promised in return for the money? Had he bought the government's contract to build the transcontinental railway?

Investigations into what came to be known as the "Pacific Scandal" revealed that Cartier had promised Hugh Allan the contract to build and run the railway in exchange for money to fund the Conservative election campaign. The Conservative government looked very bad indeed.

DEATH AND RESIGNATION

Just as the scandal broke, Cartier died in London, England, where he had gone to seek treatment for a severe illness. Macdonald was left to defend himself alone. In November 1873, he rose in the House of Commons. His speech was magnificent, but his conduct in the scandal had not been, and he was forced to resign.

The following year, a Liberal government under Alexander Mackenzie was elected. Mackenzie had no time for such grandiose schemes as a transcontinental railway. Even if he had, the country had been seized by an **economic depression** and had no money to spare.

P.E.I. Joins Confederation

In 1867, Prince Edward Island turned its back on Confederation. Islanders feared that their colony would lose its independence and gain little by joining Canada. A few years later, Islanders changed their minds. They were shouldering a heavy debt after building a railway from one end of the island to the other. Trade with the United States was dropping off. The new industrial age demanded coal to fuel factories, and P.E.I. had none.

Islanders swallowed their pride and fierce independence. On July 1, 1873, Prince Edward Island entered Confederation as the Canada's seventh province. Canada took over the Islanders' debt, promised them year-round transportation between the mainland and the island, and provided money to buy out the British landlords who owned most of the island's good agricultural land.

◀ Playback ▶

1. **Why did Prince Edward Island decide to join Confederation?**

2. **What difficulties faced the construction of an intercontinental railway across Canada?**

3. **How did Macdonald and Cartier cause the Pacific Scandal? Did they make the right decision?**

**Building the Canadian
Pacific Railway, 1884**

THE NATIONAL POLICY

The Pacific Scandal brought John A. Macdonald down, but he was far from out. In 1878, his Conservative Party won the election with its promise to end the depression with a new national policy. The policy embodied Macdonald's vision for the country: a railway that linked the provinces from sea to sea; thousands of settlers to open the West; and trade tariffs to protect Canadian businesses.

The Railway

In 1881, the transcontinental railway was put back on track when the government of Canada signed a contract with Canadian Pacific Railway Company. In return, the company would get $25 million, 10 million hectares of land, and control of western transportation to the United States for 20 years.

"Until that road is built, this dominion is a mere geographical expression and not one great dominion. Until bound by that iron link, we are not a dominion in fact."
— JOHN A. MACDONALD

"We are going to tie the oceans together … This bill is my pride and joy."
— GEORGE-ÉTIENNE CARTIER
INTRODUCING THE BILL TO BUILD A RAILWAY

"An act of insane recklessness."

"One of the most foolish things that could be imagined."

"A preposterous proposition."
— OPPONENTS OF THE RAILWAY

Railroad Navvies

The dangerous and back-breaking work of building a ribbon of steel across the country was in the hands of heroic railroad workers, called "navvies." They faced their greatest challenges in the Canadian Shield that covered northern Ontario and the mighty Rockies in the West. They blasted tunnels out of rock and built bridges across rivers and deep gorges.

About 15 000 Chinese labourers were hired because they were cheap, they worked hard, and the government felt their deaths didn't count. Their jobs tended to be the most dangerous ones on the British Columbia section: constructing tunnels, working on narrow ledges above gorges, and using explosives. It is said that one Chinese navvy died for every mile of track laid.

In 1885, when Donald A. Smith drove the last spike in the CPR in British Columbia's Monashee Mountains, the dominion's first major project was complete.

Telling Their Stories

HOMESTEADING WOMEN

Watch *Canada: A People's History*, Episode 10, "That Little Wooden Box" (10:33:48 to 10:39:23) to hear the stories of Jennie Plaxton, Louisa McDougall, Hilda Kirkland, and Mary Louisa Cummins. Write a letter or a diary entry, in role, as one of these people, telling why you have chosen to come to the West, what you hope for, what difficulties you face, and whether or not you want to stay.

Surveyors marked out property lines on their maps. A one-square-mile plot contained 640 acres and was called a section. Six sections made a township. An address on a surveyor's map in the North West was as exact as a street address in Montreal.

More Settlers

Prairie land stretched west and north from Winnipeg, the capital of the new province of Manitoba. The soils were fertile. Grasses grew as far west as the eye could see. Anxious to attract new settlers, the government of Canada offered free land in the West. It was an invitation that was hard to resist for people pushed to leave their homes by poverty, hunger, and unemployment. The promise of owning their own land pulled them towards the Canadian West.

In a few short years after 1870, thousands of settlers from eastern Canada and Europe arrived at Red River, then headed north and west to find new farmland and new opportunities. What happened here would take place again and again as the new railway made it possible to reach the unbroken lands of the North West.

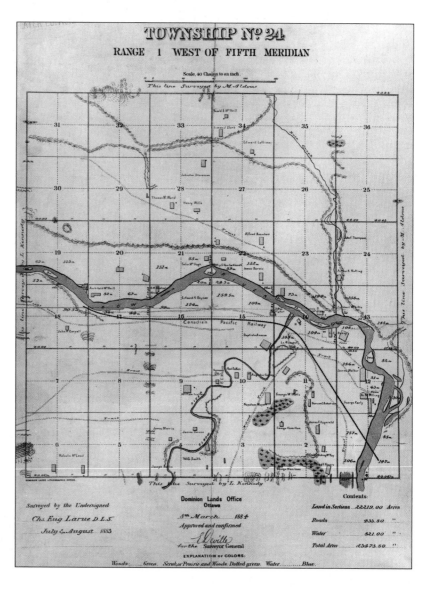

THE IMMIGRANTS

Gimli, Manitoba, in the 1870s

Icelanders

The Push

The early 1870s were terrible years for Icelanders. Erupting volcanoes showered villages with rock and ash. An epidemic killed thousands of sheep and threw farmers into poverty. Poor weather ruined crops, and earthquakes destroyed homes. Poverty, starvation, and fear drove many people to search for a better land.

The Pull

In 1875, 235 Icelanders stepped ashore at Lake Winnipeg, ready to break the land and settle in what they called Nyja Island—New Iceland. Over the next few years, more Icelanders arrived in the settlement. By this time, there were other settlers in the region, the railway ran west, supplies were easier to come by, and life became a bit easier.

Mennonites from Russia

The Push

Mennonites were pushed from their homes in Russia when the Czar took away their right to follow their religious beliefs. The Mennonites believed in non-violence, in living together in their own farming communities with their own schools and traditions, and in speaking their native German language. The Czar demanded that the Mennonites speak Russian and that their sons enlist in the army. They had only two choices: cooperate or leave.

The Pull

The government of Canada promised the Mennonites large parcels of land where they could set up farming communities and run their own schools. Their sons would not have to serve in the army. Between 1874 and 1880, 7500 Mennonites moved to Manitoba and went to work clearing and breaking land, building houses, and planting crops.

Buying Canadian

The third part of Macdonald's National Policy called for trade among the provinces and territories. But it would be a difficult idea to sell in the North West. Both Canada and the United States were in an economic depression. American companies were sending their manufactured goods north, dumping them in Canada at prices that were lower than Canadian goods. No matter how much a farmer in the West believed in Canada, he needed to buy his supplies at the lowest price possible.

In Macdonald's vision, people in the North West would buy products manufactured in eastern Canada and send their grain and other farm products back east to feed the cities. To make it work, the government decided to build walls against American goods with **tariffs**, or taxes, on imports and exports. It increased tariffs on manufactured American goods, which made buying Canadian products cheaper. It reduced tariffs on raw materials coming into Canada, so that manufacturers with factories in the eastern provinces could buy their materials more cheaply.

After his re-election in 1878, Prime Minister John A. Macdonald travelled the country promoting his National Policy. The only way to save Confederation, he argued, was for the government to build a transcontinental railway, open up the West to settlers, and impose tariffs on American goods to protect Canada's "infant industries."

INTO THE FUTURE

By 1880, the future in the Canadian West seemed set: more settlers, more farms, a railway to carry people and goods across the land, and a policy to ensure that Canada would prosper.

But there were problems in the North West. Surveyors began to slice the land into square sections for settlers, ignoring the boundaries of the long, narrow river lots of the Métis. The Métis sent a petition to the government of the North West, asking that the ownership of their land be confirmed. Their request was heard and then ignored.

The Native people of the North West were facing starvation. In the treaties they had signed, the Canadian government had promised them food and help in setting up farms. The government failed to send enough supplies to the Native reserves, and people were hungry. New settlers were fencing land, and the Native people were told to stop hunting and fishing where the newcomers were homesteading. By the 1880s, the Native people were disillusioned with the deal they thought they had made with the Canadian government.

What would the future hold for the people of the North West? How would they deal with their changing lives and the government's broken promises? The next decade would bring some violent answers.

Métis traders and their families set up camp, late 1870s

◀ Playback ▶

1. **What brought settlers to the Canadian West?**

2. **How was land surveyed in the West? What problems did this cause?**

3. **What is a tariff? Why do governments impose tariffs on imported goods?**

4. **Predict how the Métis and Native people would react to the government's broken promises. If you were Prime Minister Macdonald, what would you do to fix the problems?**

The Back Story

When Canada began opening the West in the 1850s, life changed for the people who lived there. Between 1880 and 1890, even more dramatic changes came to British Columbia and the North West.

The Goal

In small groups, prepare a report on one of several possible topics about change in British Columbia and the North West between 1880 and 1890.

The Steps

1. With your group, choose one of the following topics:
   - The building of the railway—how it changed the North West and B.C.
   - Settlement of the West—the settlers, the land, and the changes
   - The Métis and a new rebellion—the role of the Métis and Louis Riel in the Northwest Rebellion of 1885
   - The First Nations—the changes that spelled the end of their traditional way of life and the beginning of life on reserves.
2. Research your topic using this book and other sources, including the Internet.
3. Prepare an oral report about your topic. Your report should also include a portfolio of quotations, letters, drawings, photographs, maps, and charts that support your conclusions.
4. Present your report to the class. Be prepared to explain your conclusions and answer questions.

Evaluating Your Work

As you work, keep these criteria in mind. Be sure to:
- work cooperatively in your group
- review a range of resources and keep an accurate set of notes
- gather both visual and written material
- plan the oral presentation and the portfolio
- present a clear, well-organized oral report
- present an attractive, organized, detailed portfolio using images and quotations.

Report on Change in the West

CHAPTER 5

Fast Forward

Calgary, Alberta

Today, skyscrapers tower over Vancouver's busy harbour. Highways cross the rivers where fur-trading posts once stood. Cattle graze in fields where buffalo used to run. Where there were forests, now there are cities. A trip across the West that once took months on horseback, then days by train, now takes just hours by air.

Yet the questions at the centre of this book are as important today as they were in 1870. What rights do newcomers have? Are they different from the rights of people whose families have lived in Canada a long time? How can rights be protected?

THE CHANGING WEST

A hundred years ago, people living in the West listened for the mournful whistle of trains carrying settlers and lumber, food, and furniture across the prairies and through the mountains. Now, trains no longer play such a big part of life in the West.

Trains still transport wheat and coal east to the Great Lakes ports or west to Vancouver and Prince Rupert, but many other products, such as fruits, vegetables, clothes, and cars, are shipped by trucks on busy highways. Most people travel by car or by plane. Why do you think these changes have happened?

Immigrants who settled on the Canadian prairies between 1890 and 1910 homesteaded and became farmers. They ploughed thousands of hectares of land, grew wheat and other grains, and raised cattle. In British Columbia, immigrants came to work as lumberjacks and miners. They built roads and towns and opened up the interior of the province. Most of the early immigrants came from Europe, and a few came from Asia.

Today, most people in the West live in cities. Most immigrants start their new lives in cities where they can find work, homes, and communities. Can you suggest how this has changed the West? Now, the largest number of immigrants come from countries in Asia, such as China and India. How has this changed the West?

An abandoned mining town in British Columbia

A busy street in Vancouver's Chinatown

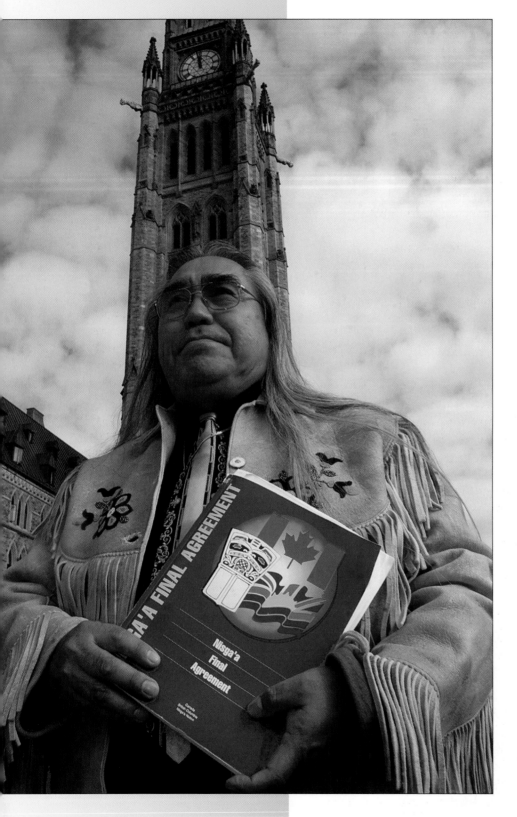

THE CHANGING WORLD OF FIRST NATIONS

More than a hundred years after Canada moved into the West, Native people are still striving to regain rights and land. Some First Nations want land returned to them. Others want rights to fish and hunt on their traditional territories. Many want compensation for the years that they spent in **residential schools**, where they were not allowed to speak their own language or learn their own traditions.

The Treaty Process

When First Nations on the prairies signed treaties with the British Crown or the Canadian government, many gave up much of their traditional lands in return for food, supplies, and financial assistance. Today, some Native groups think the treaties were unfair and are fighting in court for more rights. The biggest battles are in British Columbia and the North, where very few treaties were signed.

In 1887, representatives of the Nisga'a First Nations travelled from northwestern British Columbia to Victoria to ask the government to recognize their rights to their ancestral land. In 1999, more than 100 years later, a treaty was finally signed between the Nisga'a and the provincial and federal governments.

The Nisga'a Battle

The Nisga'a in northwestern British Columbia began their fight almost as soon as British Columbia took over their land.

1887 The Nisga'a send a delegation to Victoria, initiating a legal land claim. They are snubbed.

1913 After a number of delegations and requests for a treaty and lands are ignored, the Nisga'a send a petition to the British Privy Council, asking for land and rights.

1955 The four clans of the Nisga'a unite in the Nisga'a Tribal Council to pursue their claim.

1969 The Nisga'a file the claims known as the Calder Case, named after Nisga'a chief Frank Calder, the first Aboriginal person elected to a Canadian legislature, in 1949.

1973 The Calder Case reaches the Supreme Court of Canada. Though the court is divided, it does rule that the Nisga'a possess some land and other rights.

1990 The Nisga'a begin formal negotiations with the provincial and federal governments.

1997 The case known as Delgamuukw, filed by the Gitksan and Wet'suwet'en of northwestern British Columbia, reaches the Supreme Court of Canada. The court acknowledges that the concept of aboriginal title to land exists, and encourages the First Nations and the government to reach a negotiated settlement of land claims.

1999 The Nisga'a reach a treaty arrangement with the federal and provincial governments. The treaty is later ratified by all sides. It gives the Nisga'a land, cash, money for the development of fisheries, rights to natural resources, and a form of self-government. The Nisga'a give up their exemption from taxation and agree to make no further title claims.

First Nation protestor blockading a road in northern B.C.

Time and Louis Riel

On November 15, 1885, Louis Riel was hanged for treason. But his death did not end the story. The Métis thought he was a hero and a martyr because he died fighting for their rights. Many people in Quebec also thought of Riel as a hero, who fought for Canadians to have the right to speak and be educated in the French language.

Manitobans saw Riel as the founder of Manitoba. Many westerners saw Riel as the first— though far from the last—to fight for the rights of the West to make its own decisions.

As time passed, more and more people began to think of Riel as a hero, not a traitor. A statue to Riel was erected outside the Manitoba Legislative Buildings. On March 11, 1992, the Canadian House of Commons voted unanimously to recognize Riel's "unique and historic role as a founder of Manitoba and his contribution in the development of Confederation." They saluted Riel for "his deep devotion to his people and his willingness to pay the ultimate price of his life."

Riel is now officially a Father of Confederation.

THE FUTURE AND THE WEST

Some westerns say: "We send too much tax money to Ottawa and get back too little in return." Others argue that Quebec and Ontario decide what happens in Canada. And others complain: "People in Toronto and Ottawa don't understand anything about what happens in Vancouver and Calgary. They won't listen and they don't care."

Westerners have their own ideas about changes that will give them a stronger role in Canada and more control over their own affairs. The Senate should be elected, not appointed. Then there would be more people in Ottawa speaking out for the West. The provinces should have more power over their affairs, so westerners can make decisions for the West. The government in Ottawa should send more money to the western provinces, or it should lower taxes.

Some westerners even think that it would be a good idea to separate from Canada. Some want to join the United States, and others want to set up an independent country. What do you think about these ideas?

◀ Playback ▶

1. **What changes have occurred in Canadian life over the last 100 years?**

2. **What changes have occurred in your own life? What changes have you seen in your community?**

3. **What changes do you hope to see in the future in your life, in your community, and in Canada?**

4. **Write several paragraphs describing a day in the future when the changes you would like to see have come into effect.**

The Back Story

Canada has been a country for fewer than 150 years, and its story is one of great and rapid change. Some of the most dramatic changes happened in the West. You have read about new groups of people arriving and First Nations and Métis losing their land and rights. You have read about railways being built and cities growing. Today, the West continues to change. What does change mean for you and your community?

The Goal

Create a collage that shows how the life of your family or your community has changed. The collage will have three panels, showing the past, the present, and what you think or hope will happen in the future.

The Steps

1. Decide whether you want to make your collage about the history and future of your family or your community. Consider the three essential panels of the collage: past, present, and future.
2. For each panel, make notes about what should be included. For your family, consider such things as where your ancestors lived a hundred years ago, what they wore, what they ate, how they lived, how they travelled, and where they went to school. For your community, consider what your area was like before the community existed, who lived there first, what their life was like (their food, clothing, and shelter), and how they survived.
3. Choose images, words, and artefacts, such as train or plane tickets, small tools, postage stamps, and baby clothes.
4. Assemble your collage.
5. Prepare a five-minute talk that explains your collage to the rest of the class.

Evaluating Your Work

These are the criteria you should think about as you complete your work. Your work should:
- demonstrate information about past, present, and future
- show important events and changes in the three panels
- represent accurately the changes in the life of your family or community
- be interesting and well designed
- be unique.

History in Action

Change for You and Your Community

Glossary

Cariboo A region in the southern interior of British Columbia, with the Pacific Ocean to the west and the Cariboo Mountains to the east, where gold was discovered along the Fraser River in 1858.

Denominational schools Schools that have a religious charter.

Economic depression A period of hardship when businesses go broke and people lose their jobs. In the worldwide depression that lasted from the early 1870s to the early 1890s, Canada's trade in resources and goods with Britain and the U.S. dropped, factories closed down, and unemployment rose.

49th parallel The line of latitude that marks the border between Canada and the United States.

Indian Act The Canadian law passed in 1876 that defined the status of First Nations people and how the reserves were to be run and governed. The Act made all First Nations wards of the federal government, which meant they were to be treated as minors without the full rights of citizenship.

Manifest Destiny An American belief from the 1840s which stated that it was part of God's plan that the United States should control all of North America.

Monopoly Total control of the buying or selling of a resource or product by a company or person.

Northwest Rebellion The 1885 rebellion of Métis and Native people against the Canadian government, which had failed to recognize Métis rights and to keep its treaty promises to the Native people. Battles were fought in present-day Saskatchewan. The Canadian government charged Louis Riel, the leader of the rebellion, with treason and ordered his execution by hanging.

Pemmican A nutritious food made from dried buffalo meat and mixed with fat and berries. Native people carried it on long hunting trips and sold it to fur traders.

Provisional government A temporary government. A provisional government was set up by the Métis in Red River in 1869 to keep law and order during negotiations with Canada about joining Confederation.

Reserves Land owned by the Canadian government that is set aside, or reserved, for First Nations.

Residential schools Boarding schools run by churches, and approved by the Canadian government, to educate Native children from the 1870s to the 1970s. Often separated from their families for years, these children were not allowed to speak their own language or follow their traditions. Many were abused physically and emotionally.

Rights Basic freedoms that people are entitled to, based on custom or law.

Secede To withdraw or separate from a country or group.

Self-government A system of government in which Aboriginal people have more control over their affairs, such as education, housing, and community development.

Smallpox A highly contagious disease that is characterized by very high fever and skin blisters.

Survey To measure land and define boundaries. Surveyors used chains that had 100 links and were 66 feet long to measure land in the West.

Tariffs Taxes that a government sets on goods imported from outside the country. Tariffs make the price of goods from outside the country higher than the price of the same goods inside the country, which increases the markets and profits of the country's producers and manufacturers.

Treaty An agreement reached by negotiation. In the late 1800s, many First Nations gave up their traditional territories to the Canadian government in exchange for reserve land and promises of government assistance.

Index

Credits

Cover top: Library and Archives Canada, C-11021; bottom left: CP/Fred Chartrand; bottom right: Roy Ooms/Masterfile; Page 1 Library and Archives Canada, C- 11021; Page 2 top left: Glenbow Archives, NA-325-4; top right: Library and Archives Canada, e002414863; bottom: Library and Archives Canada, C-095320; Page 3 top left: *In Commemoration, No. 2. — Wolseley, the Soldier*, McCord Museum of Canadian History, Montreal; top middle: Glenbow Archives, NA-2631-1; top right: Library and Archives Canada, C-002078; bottom: map, Paperglyphs; Page 4 Library and Archives Canada, C-119982; Page 5 map, Paperglyphs; Page 6 CBC *Canada: A People's History*; Page 7 John Mardon; Page 8 map, Paperglyphs; Page 9 map, Paperglyphs; Page 10 Glenbow Archives, NA-325-4; Page 11 *The Situation*, McCord Museum of Canadian History, Montreal; Page 12 Library and Archives Canada, C-079903; Page 13 Library and Archives Canada, PA-011337; Page 14 Library and Archives Canada, PA-012854; Page 15 Glenbow Archives, NA-2631-1; Page 16 Library and Archives Canada, e002414863; Page 17 left: © Crown, Reproduced with permission of the Department of Justice; right: CBC, *Canada: A People's History*; Page 18 *In Commemoration, No. 2. — Wolseley, the Soldier*, McCord Museum of Canadian History, Montreal; Page 19 Library and Archives Canada, C-011782; Page 20 Library and Archives Canada, e002414863; Page 21 Provincial Archives of Victoria, B.C.; Page 22 Provincial Archives of Victoria, B.C.; Page 23 top: Canada Museum of Civilization; bottom: Provincial Archives of Victoria, B.C.; Page 24 top: Library and Archives, PA-061940; bottom: BC Archives, F-02310; Page 25 Provincial Archives of BC; Page 26 BC Archives, A-01227; Page 27 Library and Archives Canada, C-029180; Page 28 *The Tyee Potlatch* by James Gerrais, British Columbia Archives, PDP00714; Page 29 BC Archives, 761; Page 30 *Journeys of Exploration, Growth of a Nation Series*

(Fitzhenry & Whiteside, 1995); Page 32 Library and Archives Canada, PA-025397; Page 33 BC Archives, B09764; Page 34 BC Archives, B09764; Page 35 Library and Archives Canada, C- 11021; Page 36 G89.16.4; Courtesy of the Provincial Museum of Alberta, Edmonton, Alberta; Page 37 Library and Archives Canada, PA-066544; Page 38 Glenbow Archives, NA-2347-1; Page 39 Library and Archives Canada, C-11553; Page 40 *Fort Whoop-up, Alberta*, by G.M. Dawson, 1881. Reproduced with the permission of the Minister of Public Works and Government Services Canada, 2006 and Courtesy of Natural Resources Canada, Geological Survey of Canada; Page 43 Glenbow Archives, NA-716-19; Page 44 top: Glenbow Archives, NA-3811-2a; bottom: Glenbow Archives, NA-2206-1; Page 45 Glenbow Archives, WA-40-1; Page 47 CBC, *Canada: A People's History*; Page 48 Glenbow Archives, WA-40-1; Page 49 Library and Archives Canada, C-003693; Page 50 from left to right; Library and Archives Canada, C-12216; *Hon. George Etienne Cartier, politician, Montreal, QC, 1865*, McCord Museum of Canadian History, Montreal; Library and Archives Canada, C-002078; Page 52 Glenbow Archives, NA-448-9; Page 53 *Chinese work gang on the C.P.R., Glacier Park, BC, 1889*, McCord Museum of Canadian History, Montreal; Page 54 top: CBC, *Canada: A People's History*; bottom: Glenbow Archives, NA-3487-9; Page 55 Courtesy of the New Icelandic Heritage Museum; Page 57 Library and Archives Canada, C-004164; Page 58 Library and Archives Canada, C-004164; Page 59 Roy Ooms/Masterfile; Page 60 top: Glenbow Archives, NA-664-3; bottom: Gloria H. Chomica/Masterfile; Page 61 top: © Gunter Marx Photography/CORBIS; bottom: Andrew Wenzel/Masterfile; Page 62 CP/Fred Chartrand; Page 63 top: John Mardon; bottom: Kamloops Daily News/Murray Mitchell; Page 65 Library and Archives Canada, C-002048.

Reviewers

Kathryn Brownell, Terry Fox School, Toronto, Ontario

Manny Calisto, West St. Paul School, West St. Paul, Manitoba

Greer Coe, Montague Intermediate School, Montague, Prince Edward Island

Rick Elliott, John Buchan School, Toronto, Ontario

Sheri Epstein, Langstaff High School, Thornhill, Ontario

Christine Greene, Avalon East School Board, St. John's, Newfoundland

Joanne Wheeler, St. Margaret School, Calgary, Alberta